Introduction to Geometric Shapes

Geometry Books for Kids

Children's Math Books

BABY PROFESSOR

EDUCATION KIDS

A SHAPE is a form of a thing or its outside surface or outline.

TRIANGLE

Practice Tracing

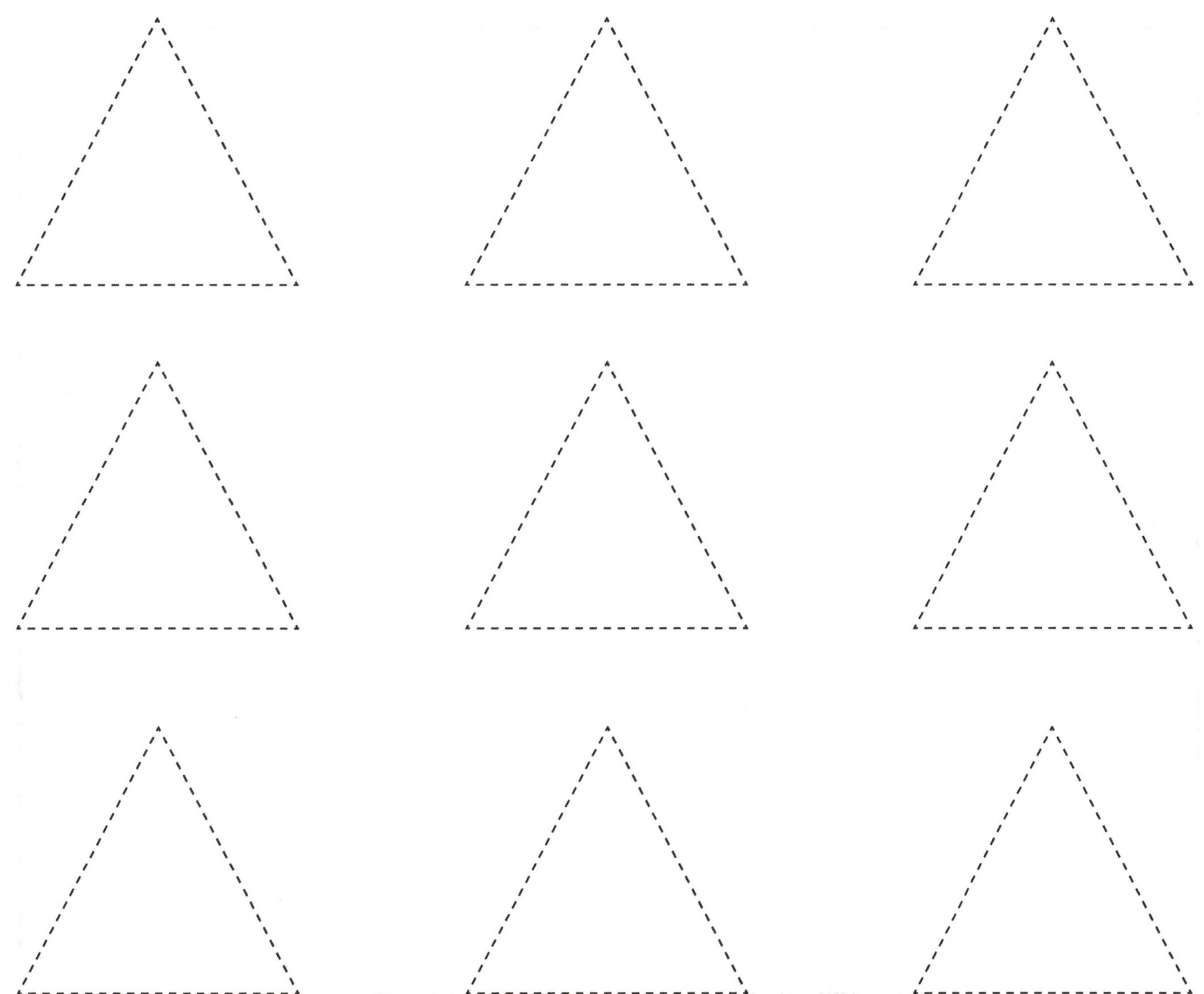

Do it your own!

Triangle

Look around you, draw any **triangle** object you have seen.

SQUARE

Practice Tracing

Do it your own!

Square

Look around you, draw any square object you have seen.

DIAMOND

Practice Tracing

Do it your own!

Diamond

Look around you, draw any diamond object you have seen.

CIRCLE

Practice Tracing

Do it your own!

Circle

Look around you, draw any circle object you have seen.

STAR

Practice Tracing

Do it your own!

Star

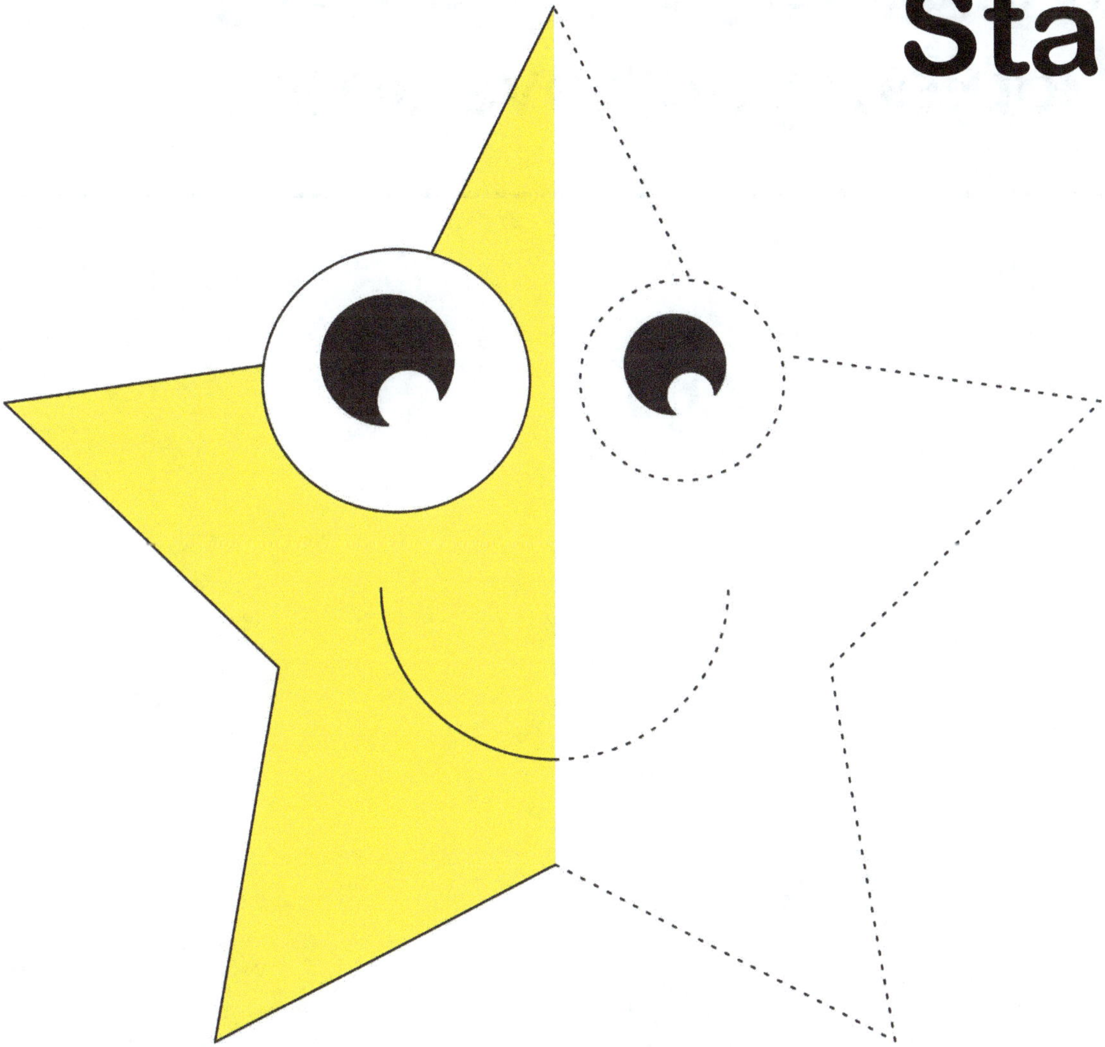

Look around you, draw any star object you have seen.

RECTANGLE

Practice Tracing

Do it your own!

Rectangle

Look around you, draw any rectangle object you have seen.

HEART

Practice Tracing

Do it your own!

Heart

Look around you, draw any heart object you have seen.

ELLIPSE

Practice Tracing

Do it your own!

Ellipse

Look around you, draw any ellipse object you have seen.

PENTAGON

Practice Tracing

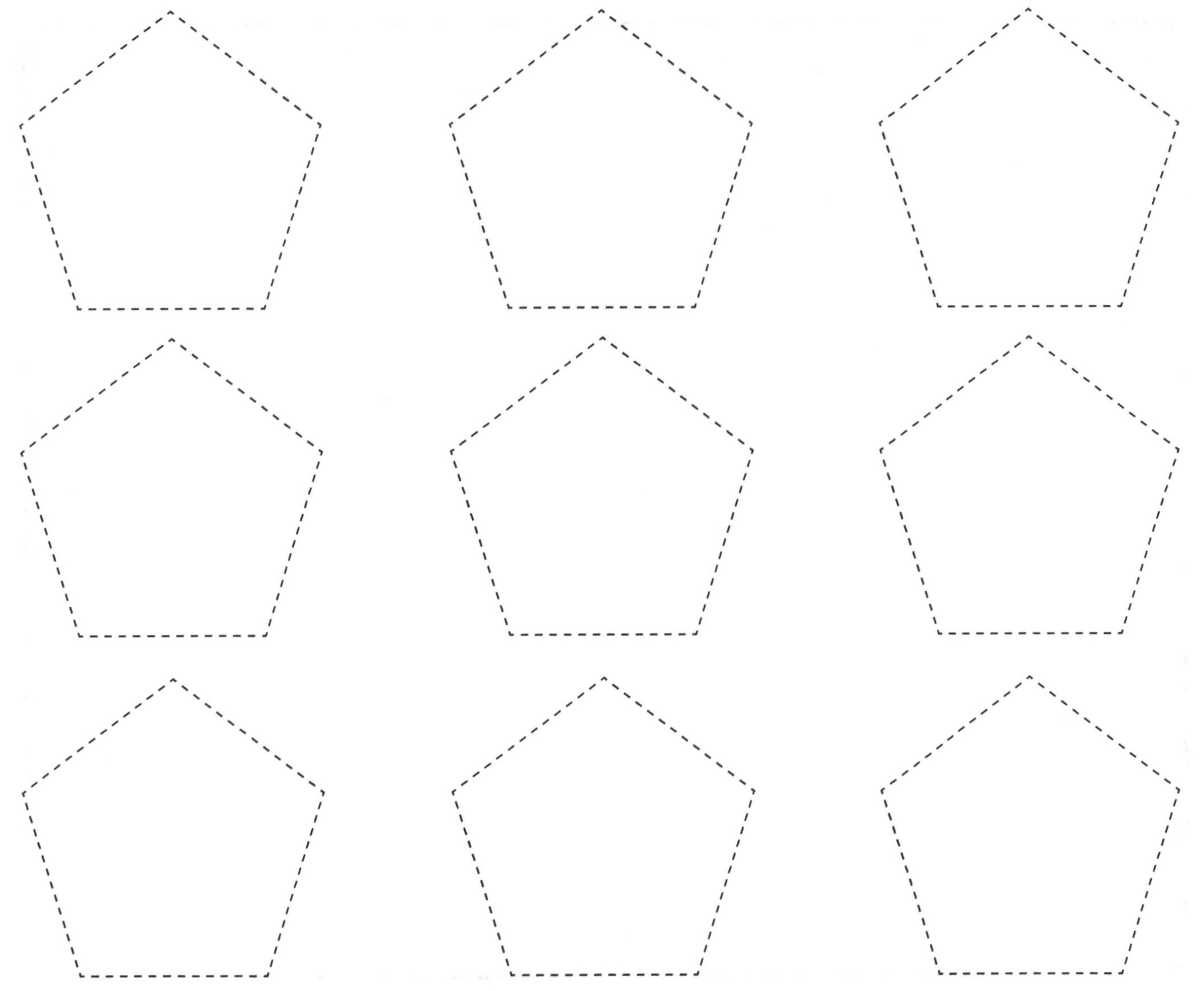

Do it your own!

Pentagon

Look around you, draw any **pentagon** object you have seen.

TRAPEZIUM

Practice Tracing

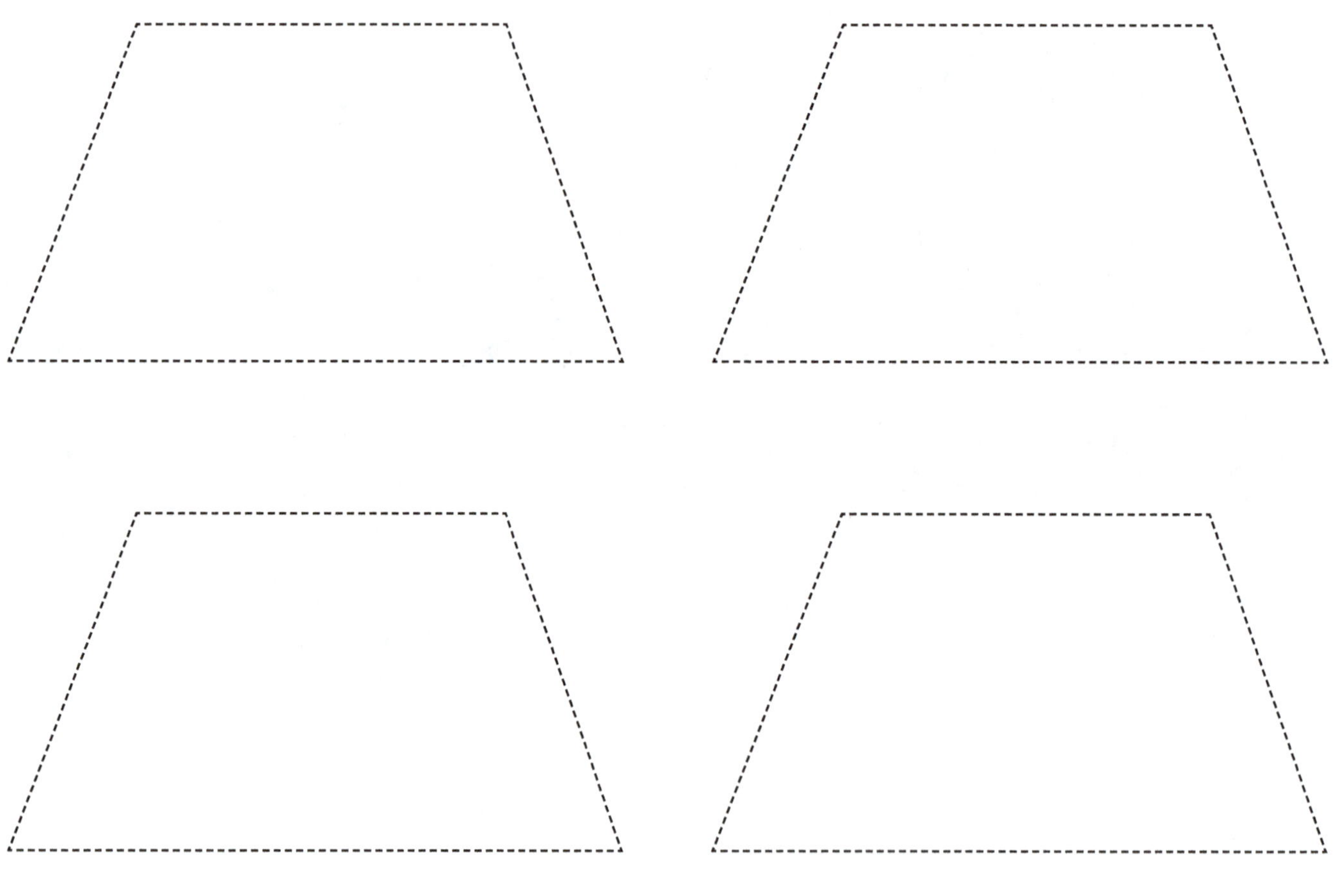

Do it your own!

Trapezium

Look around you, draw any **trapezium** object you have seen.

OCTAGON

Practice Tracing

Do it your own!

Look around you, draw any octagon object you have seen.

HEPTAGON

Practice Tracing

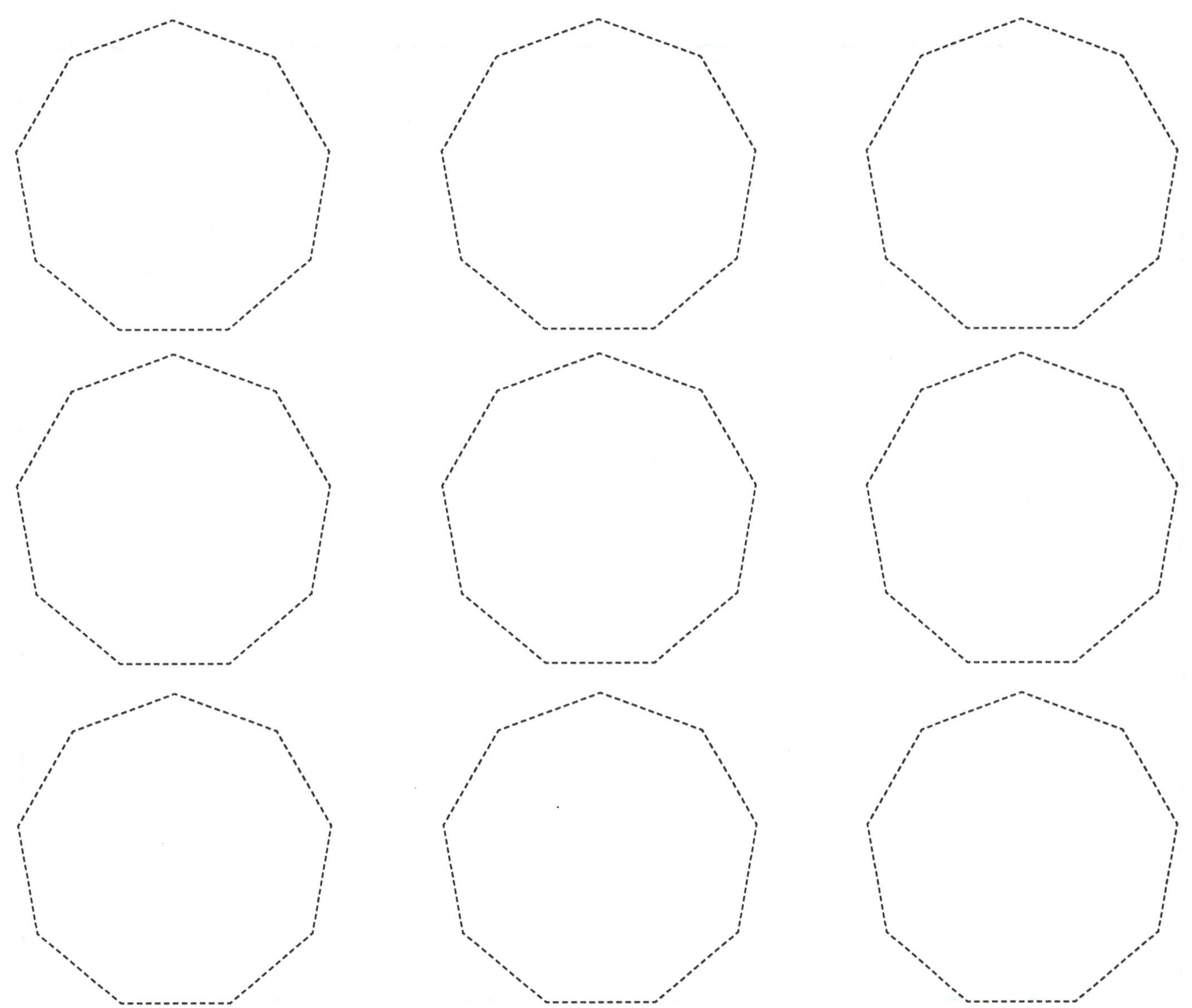

Do it your own!

Look around you, draw any heptagon object you have seen.

Color the heart shapes with red.

Color the square shapes with blue.